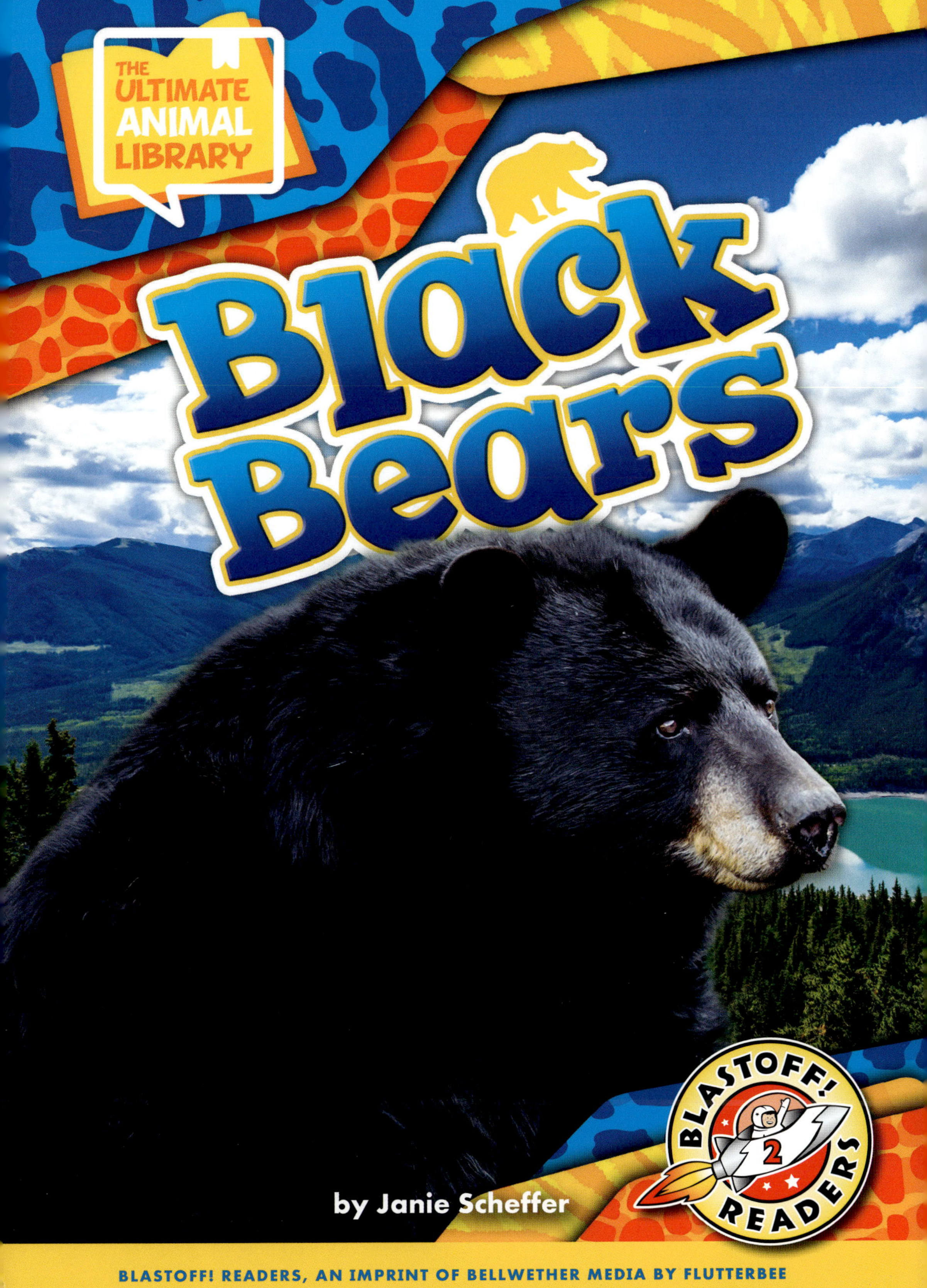

BLASTOFF! READERS, AN IMPRINT OF BELLWETHER MEDIA BY FLUTTERBEE

Blastoff! Readers are carefully developed by literacy experts to build reading stamina and move students toward fluency by combining standards-based content with developmentally appropriate text.

Level 1 provides the most support through repetition of high-frequency words, light text, predictable sentence patterns, and strong visual support.

Level 2 offers early readers a bit more challenge through varied sentences, increased text load, and text-supportive special features.

Level 3 advances early-fluent readers toward fluency through increased text load, less reliance on photos, advancing concepts, longer sentences, and more complex special features.

★ **Blastoff! Universe**

Reading Level

Grade K

Grades 1–3

Grade 4

This edition first published in 2026 by Bellwether Media, Inc.

For information regarding permission, write to Bellwether Media, Inc., Attention: Permissions Department, 3500 American Blvd W, Suite 150, Bloomington, MN 55431.

Library of Congress Cataloging-in-Publication Data is available at www.loc.gov or upon request from the publisher.

ISBN: 9798893047899 (hardcover)
ISBN: 9798893048896 (ebook)

Editor: Elizabeth Neuenfeldt   Designer: Brittany McIntosh

Printed in the United States of America, North Mankato, MN.

Table of Contents

What Are Black Bears?

Black bears are **mammals**. These bears are not always black! Many live in North America. Others live in parts of Asia.

American Black Bear Report

Black bears have big bodies. Males are bigger than females.

Some males are over 6 feet (2 meters) long! They can weigh up to 900 pounds (408 kilograms).

Many black bears have black fur. Others are grayish or brown. Some have white marks.

They have thick layers
of fur to stay warm.

Black bears have round ears. They have **curved** claws to climb, dig, and find food.

They can smell very well. They can smell food from over 1 mile (1.6 kilometers) away!

Spot a Black Bear
round ears
thick layers
of fur
curved
claws

Strong Climbers!

grassland

Black bears live alone in forests, **grasslands**, and mountains.

They are strong climbers. They rest, eat, and play in trees.

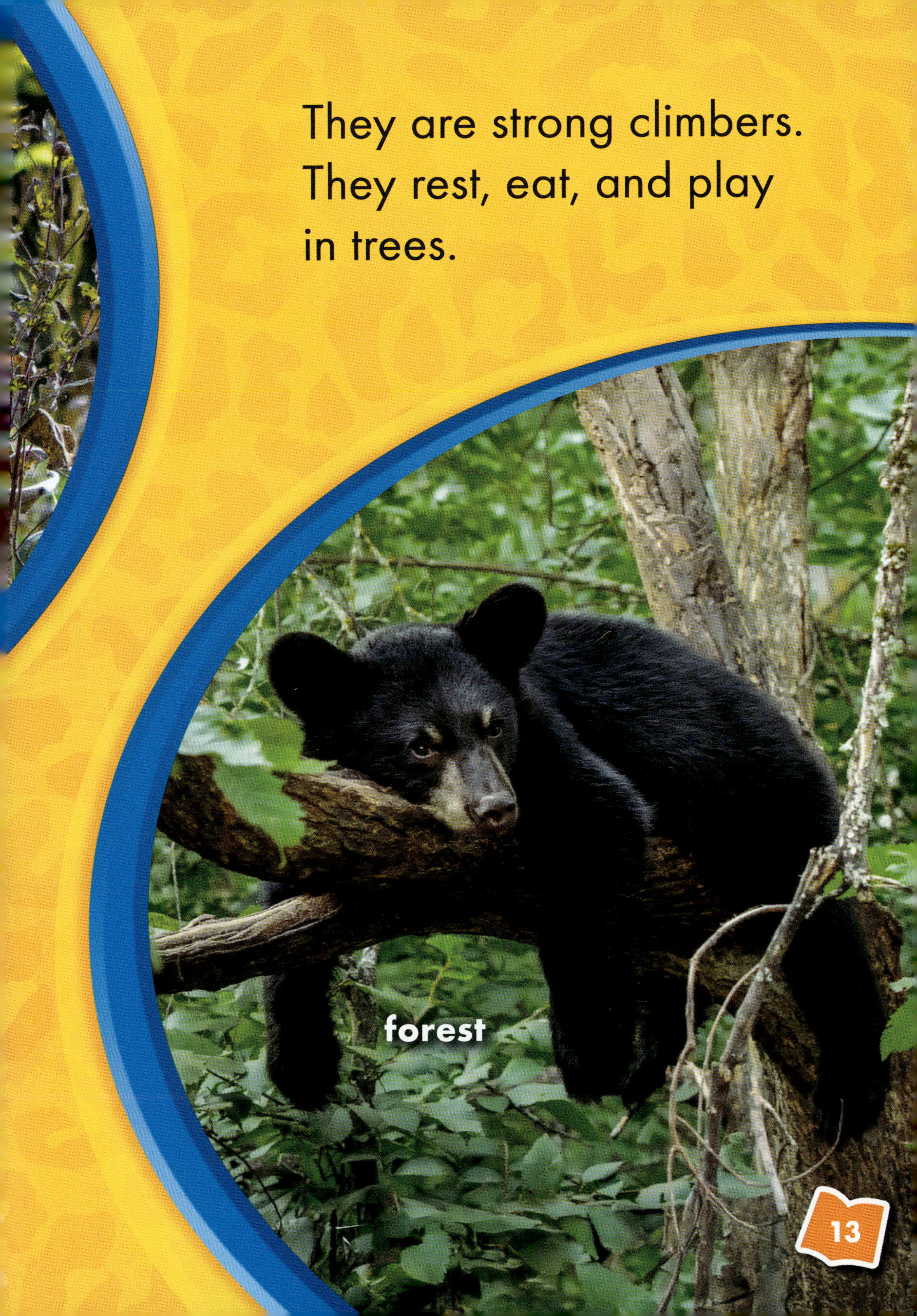

Black bears are **omnivores**. They mostly eat plants, berries, and **insects**.

Black Bear Food Web

wolves

plants

berries

insects

They are hunted by wolves.
They climb trees to stay safe
from **predators**!

Most black bears **hibernate** in winter. They rest in **dens**.

den

They eat a lot before they hibernate. They build fat to stay warm!

Growing Up

Female black bears give birth to one to four **cubs**. This happens every two to three years.

Cubs are born **blind**. They drink mom's milk.

cub

Cubs eat plants after a few months. They stay with mom for about two years.

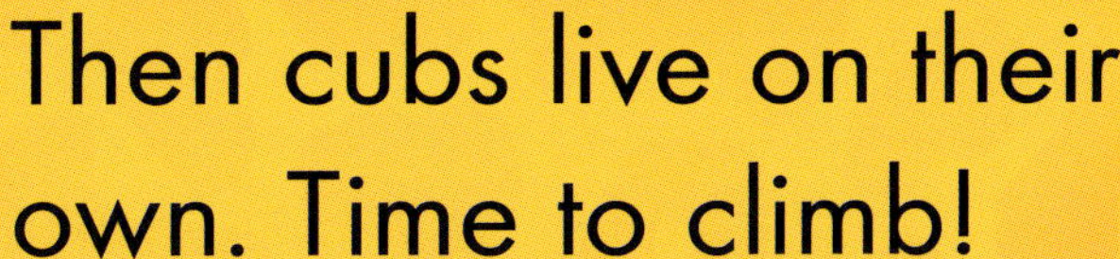

Then cubs live on their own. Time to climb!

Life of a Black Bear

Name of Babies

cubs

Number of Babies

1 to 4

Time Spent with Mom

Glossary

blind—unable to see

cubs—baby black bears

curved—having a bend

dens—sheltered places

grasslands—lands covered with grasses and other soft plants with few bushes or trees

hibernate—to spend the winter in a deep sleep

insects—small animals with six legs and bodies divided into three parts

mammals—warm-blooded animals that have backbones and feed their young milk

omnivores—animals that eat both plants and animals

predators—animals that hunt other animals for food

To Learn More

AT THE LIBRARY

Hall, Alex. *Bears.* Mendota Heights, Minn.: North Star Editions, 2025.

London, Martha. *Black Bear Hibernation.* Minneapolis, Minn.: Bearport Publishing Company, 2024.

Schmitz, Chris. *Black Bear or Grizzly Bear?: A Compare and Contrast Book.* Mt. Pleasant, S.C.: Arbordale Publishing, 2023.

ON THE WEB

FACTSURFER

Factsurfer.com gives you a safe, fun way to find more information.

1. Go to www.factsurfer.com.
2. Enter "black bears" into the search box and click 🔍.
3. Select your book cover to see a list of related content.

Index

The images in this book are reproduced through the courtesy of: Glass and Nature, front cover (bear); BGSmith, front cover (background), pp. 2-3, 14-15; Anan Kaewkhammul, pp. 3, 18; Holly Kuchera, p. 4; All Canada Photos/ Alamy Stock Photo, p. 6; Mircea Costina, p. 7; Don Johnston_MA/ Alamy Stock Photo, p. 8; Volodymyr Burdiak, pp. 9, 15 (wolves); Various images, p. 10; John Morrison, pp. 10-11; Svetlana Foote, pp. 11, 23; K Quinn Ferris, p. 12; PVminer2, p. 13; Ben McMurtray, p. 15 (bear); Wirestock Creators, p. 15 (plants); Emils Lukso, p. 15 (berries); Jay Ondreicka, p. 15 (insects); Carlos Carreno/ Getty Images, p. 16; WendyCotie, p. 17; Debbie Steinhausser, pp. 18-19; blickwinkel/ Alamy Stock Photo, p. 20; Robert Harding Video, p. 21.